Anonymous

The solicitorship to the Worshipful Company of

Clothworkers

Testimonials of Mr. Herbert Walter Nelson

Anonymous

The solicitorship to the Worshipful Company of Clothworkers
Testimonials of Mr. Herbert Walter Nelson

ISBN/EAN: 9783337283551

Printed in Europe, USA, Canada, Australia, Japan

Cover: Foto ©Andreas Hilbeck / pixelio.de

More available books at **www.hansebooks.com**

THE

SOLICITORSHIP

TO THE

Worshipful Company of Clothworkers.

•

𝕮𝖊𝖘𝖙𝖎𝖒𝖔𝖓𝖎𝖆𝖑𝖘

OF

MR. HERBERT WALTER NELSON.

INDEX.

- ◆ -

From the Attorney-General, Sir JOHN DUKE COLERIDGE,
Knight, Q.C., &c.,

M.P. FOR EXETER.

WESTMINSTER HALL,

1st September, 1873.

MY DEAR SIR,

I have very great pleasure in testifying to your perfect fitness for the post you are seeking from the Clothworkers' Company. I have known you in business many years, both on the Western Circuit and in London, and have no doubt whatever that you will discharge, with entire satisfaction to the Company, all the duties of the office if they should see fit to elect you.

Believe me to be,

Faithfully yours,

J. D. COLERIDGE.

H. W. NELSON, Esq.

From SIR JOHN BURGESS KARSLAKE. Kt., Q.C., &c.

HELMSDALE,

SUTHERLAND, N.B.,

31st August, 1873.

DEAR SIR,

I am ashamed to find that your letter, dated the 13th, which, after much wandering, reached me here is still unanswered. From my knowledge of your professional character and reputation I have no doubt that you would very effectually discharge the duties of Solicitor to the Clothworkers' Company.

I remain, dear Sir,

Yours truly,

JOHN B. KARSLAKE.

From **W. B. GLASSE, Esqre., Q.C.**

LINCOLN'S INN,

18th August, 1873.

DEAR SIR,

From what I have had the opportunity of seeing you in the conduct of business, I have no hesitation in expressing my opinion that you are thoroughly competent to discharge the duties of Solicitor to the Clothworkers' Company.

Believe me,

Truly yours,

W. B. GLASSE.

H. W. NELSON, Esq.

From **CLEMENT MILWARD, Esqre., Q.C.**

FAIRTHORN, BOILEY, HANTS,

21st August, 1873.

GENTLEMEN,

I take the liberty of saying that I have known Mr. NELSON in business for several years, and entertain a high opinion of his ability, and am confident that he would be found thoroughly efficient for the Office of Solicitor to your Worshipful Company.

I have the honour to be, Gentn.,

Your most humble Servt.,

CLEMENT MILWARD, Q.C.

To the WORSHIPFUL
THE CLOTHWORKERS' COMPANY.

From H. J. COLE. Esqre., Q C.

RECORDER OF PLYMOUTH AND DEVONPORT.

August 18th, 73.

My dear Sir,

Having heard from you that you are a Candidate for the office of Solicitor to the Worshipful Company of Clothworkers, I have much pleasure in bearing my testimony to your high qualifications for that office. Your long connection with business in the City of London, your extensive knowledge of Mercantile Law and Conveyancing, together with your high personal character, must, I am sure, render you peculiarly fitted for the office you are seeking; and I feel sure that in you any public company will find a most valuable and reliable officer.

With every good wish for your success.

Believe me,

Yours very truly,

HENRY THOS. COLE.

H. W. NELSON, Esq.

From **HENRY JAMES**, Esqre., Q.C.,
M.P. FOR TAUNTON.

NEW COURT, TEMPLE,
August 12th, 1873.

MY DEAR SIR,

I have great pleasure in stating that for some years I have been constantly instructed by you in professional matters, and have had ample opportunity of judging of your ability and assiduity towards your clients.

I can with much confidence testify to your capability in every respect to discharge the duties of Solicitor to the Clothworkers' Company, and I trust you may be successful in obtaining that office.

I am, my dear Sir,
Yours very faithfully,
HENRY JAMES.

H. NELSON, Esqre.

)

From HENRY C. LOPES, Esqre.. Q.C..

RECORDER OF EXETER, AND M.P. FOR LAUNCESTON.

13th August, 1873.

ROYAL HOTEL,

BRISTOL.

MY DEAR SIR,

I understand you are seeking the appointment of Solicitor to the Clothworkers' Company. I have had many opportunities of recognizing your great energy and the legal ability you have exhibited in cases which have come before our Courts of Law, and have no hesitation in saying that I think any public company will be fortunate if they secure the services of a professional man so well qualified as yourself to do their business.

It will give me great pleasure to hear of your obtaining this appointment.

Believe me, yours very truly,

HENRY C. LOPES.

H. W. NELSON, Esq.

From C. P. BUTT. Esqre., Q.C.

129, Mount Street,
16th August, 1873.

My dear Sir,

In consequence of my not having gone Circuit, your letter did not reach me until this morning.

I wish you all success in your candidature for the office of Solicitor to the Clothworkers' Company. Having for some years had ample opportunity of forming an estimate of your business capacity, I have no hesitation in saying that I believe you to be in every respect qualified for the office you are seeking to obtain.

I am, dear Sir,

Yours very truly,

CHARLES P. BUTT.

H. W. Nelson, Esq.,

26, Martin's Lane.

From A. E. MILLER, Esqre. Q C.

I HAVE, for more than 16 years, had very frequent opportunities of judging of Mr. HERBERT WALTER NELSON, first as Managing Clerk to his brother, the then head of his present firm, and now the Solicitor to the Corporation of London, and afterwards as Solicitor on his own account, and I can confidently recommend him to any public body requiring the services of a skilful and energetic lawyer. As an old tenant of the Clothworkers' Company, on their Co. Derry Estates, I shall be very glad to learn that they have secured Mr. NELSON's services as their Solicitor, for though I have for some years ceased to hold their land I still retain a lively interest in their welfare and that of their town of Coleraine.

ALEX. EDW. MILLER.

LINCOLN'S INN,
14th August, 1873.

TO THE MASTERS, WARDENS, AND ASSISTANTS

OF THE CLOTHWORKERS' COMPANY.

From WATKIN WILLIAMS, Esqre., Q.C.,
M.P. FOR DENBIGH.

LONDON,
August 14th, 1873.

DEAR SIR,

It gives me much pleasure to add my testimony to that of others of your fitness for the office of Solicitor to the Clothworkers' Company. My experience of your great energy and ability satisfies me that if the Company have the good fortune to select you, you will fill the office with advantage to them and credit to yourself.

Ever yours truly,
WATKIN WILLIAMS.

II. W. NELSON, Esq.

From THE HONOURABLE A. H. THESIGER. Q.C.

August 15th, 1873.

To the Court of Assistants of the Clothworkers' Company.

Gentlemen,

Understanding that Mr. Nelson is a Candidate for the post of Solicitor to the Clothworkers' Company, I am happy to have the opportunity of testifying my belief in his fitness in every respect for the post which he seeks.

I have been often brought into contact with him in professional business, chiefly in cases where I have been engaged on the opposite side to that on which he has acted as Solicitor, and I have always observed in him the greatest energy and the most watchful attention to the interests of his clients.

> I am, Gentlemen,
> Your obedient servant,
> ALFRED HY. THESIGER.

From WILLIAM ST. JAMES WHEELHOUSE, Esqre.,
Serjeants' Inn, Barrister-at-Law,
M.P. FOR LEEDS.

MY DEAR MR. NELSON,

You ask me for a Testimonial: all I can say is soon said. If either the Worshipful Company of Cloth-workers, or indeed any such body, be desirous of obtaining at once the most efficient and the most conscientious performance of duty, it would, in my humble opinion, be utterly impossible to expect or to receive it from any human being if not from you.

I state this from as close and intimate a Parliamentary knowledge of you as any man can reasonably have, or hope to have of another; and no one knows better than I do how arduously and how effectively you can and do attend to the interests of your clientalage, in every sense of the word, at all times.

Your note was addressed to me in Serjeants' Inn, and, having followed me to Leeds, accounts for the day's delay.

Wishing you every success, believe me to be,

Yours sincerely,
W. ST. J. WHEELHOUSE.

ASSIZE COURT, LEEDS,
August 14th, 1873.

From EUGENE C. CLARKSON, Esqre., Barrister-at-Law.

3, PAPER BUILDINGS, TEMPLE,
18th August, 1873.

To THE WORSHIPFUL THE CLOTHWORKERS' COMPANY.

GENTLEMEN,

Having been given to understand that the post of Solicitor to the Clothworkers' Company is vacant, and that Mr. HERBERT WALTER NELSON is a Candidate for the appointment, I have much pleasure in stating that I have known him for many years past as a very able, experienced and energetic Solicitor, and that I believe that the interests of your Company would always receive at his hands the greatest care and attention in the event of his obtaining the appointment of Solicitor to the Company.

I am, Gentlemen,
Your most obedt. Servant,
EUGENE C. CLARKSON.

From F. A. PHILBRICK, Esqre., Barrister-at-Law,

RECORDER OF COLCHESTER.

LAMB BUILDINGS, TEMPLE,
12th August, 1873.

H. W. NELSON, ESQRE.,

DEAR SIR,

I am extremely glad to learn that you are a Candidate for the Solicitorship to the Clothworkers' Company.

From some years' experience of your qualifications, both personally as a gentleman, and professionally as a lawyer, I am sure no better Candidate could seek election, and, by a somewhat singular incident, I feel I can speak with an exceptional knowledge.

In the earlier years of my introduction to the law, I was an articled clerk some time in the office of Mr. W. RIXON, the Solicitor to the Company, and while there saw and took part in much of its business.

A practical acquaintance, therefore, with what its requirements are, enables me to speak with confidence that you would, if elected, thoroughly and efficiently discharge the duties of the office ; and I write thus, not from mere friendship, or with a view to oblige, but from a conviction of your fitness for the post, based on actual experience, and that the interests of the Company would be greatly served if they were so fortunate as to secure your services.

I trust I may hear your application has been attended with success.

I am, dear Sir,
Yours very faithfully,
FRED. A. PHILBRICK.

C. J. COTTINGHAM. Esqre., Barrister-at-Law.

LONDON,

August 19th, 1873.

DEAR SIR,

I am informed you are a Candidate for the vacant post of Solicitor to the Clothworkers' Company. An acquaintance with you of some years enables me to bear my testimony (which I do very willingly) to your fitness by ability, legal attainments, and professional standing for this or any similar appointment, and should you obtain it, I cannot doubt that you will discharge the duties attached to it with credit to yourself and satisfaction to the Company.

You have my best wishes for your success.

I am, dear Sir,
Very truly yours,
C. J. COTTINGHAM,
Barrister-at-Law, L.I.

H. W. NELSON, Esq.

.

From **FITZ OWEN J. SKINNER**, Esqre.,

Barrister-at-Law and Conveyancer.

2, New Square,
20th August, 1873.

My dear Sir,

In reply to your letter informing me that you are a Candidate for the post of Solicitor to the Clothworkers' Company, I sincerely trust you may be elected, and am confident that should you be so, the Company, in obtaining the services of a gentleman of your legal knowledge and practical experience, will have secured a most valuable officer.

Yours very truly,
FITZ OWEN J. SKINNER.

H. W. Nelson, Esq.,
26, Martin's Lane.

From I. P. INGHAM, Esqre., Barrister-at-Law.

DEAR SIR,

Being a Candidate for the vacant post of Solicitor to the Clothworkers' Company, you ask me for a testimonial. If it can in any way aid your chance of success, I have great pleasure in saying that what I have seen of your work, whether in Court or out, has always been done with great ability and unvarying courtesy.

I remain, dear Sir,

Yours truly,

I. PENROSE INGHAM.

5, King's Bench Walk, Temple,
Monday, August 18th, 1873.

.

From R. E. WEBSTER, Esqre. Barrister-at-Law.

2, PUMP COURT, TEMPLE, E.C.,
12th August, 1873.

DEAR MR. NELSON,

I am pleased to learn that you think of standing for the Solicitorship of the Clothworkers' Company, and I am most happy to be able to testify from our professional acquaintance and friendship (now extending, I am glad to remember, over some years) that no one is more thoroughly competent than yourself to discharge all the duties of the office. I sincerely hope you may be successful, as I am sure the Company will secure in you a most efficient servant. I do not know whether this letter will be of any use to you, but you are most welcome to use it.

Believe me,
Yours very truly,
R. E. WEBSTER.

W. H. NELSON, Esq

From H. B BUCKLEY, Esqre., Barrister-at-Law.

3, NEW SQUARE, LINCOLN'S INN,
18th August, 1873.

DEAR SIR,

I understand that you are a Candidate for the vacant office of Solicitor to the Clothworkers' Company.

In most heartily wishing you success in your candidature, I have great pleasure in expressing my opinion that, should you be appointed to the post, your extensive and varied practice will enable you to bring to the service of the Company a professional experience which will be of the greatest value.

From my personal experience I can testify to the careful and thorough manner in which the work of your firm is done, so far as the result of that work can be traced in the papers sent to Counsel. The clear and detailed accuracy of your instructions has made it a pleasure to deal with such papers as you have laid before me.

Believe me, dear Sir,
Very faithfully yours,
H. BURTON BUCKLEY.

H. W. NELSON, Esq.,
26, Martin's Lane,
Cannon Street.

From W. H. **BUTTERWORTH** Esqre., Special Pleader.

TEMPLE,

August 15th, 1873.

MY DEAR SIR,

I understand that you are a Candidate for the vacant office of Solicitor to the Clothworkers' Company. I know how little need you have of testimonials; but, I should, after having known you for upwards of 20 years, feel aggrieved if I were not allowed on this occasion to say that during the whole of that period I have known you professionally and otherwise, and can, with truth, declare that you are beyond question fully competent to fill the office now vacant with credit to yourself and advantage to the Company. Your success in your profession, already accomplished, will confirm my statements, if any confirmation were required.

Sincerely yours,

W. H. BUTTERWORTH,

(Special Pleader).

H. W. NELSON, Esq.

FROM

PUBLIC BODIES, LANDOWNERS,

AND OTHERS.

From the **GREAT EASTERN RAILWAY COMPANY.**

LONDON,
22nd August, 1873.

MY DEAR SIR,

With reference to your application for the Solicitorship of the Clothworkers' Company, I have much pleasure in saying that I hope you will be successful, as I am satisfied from the experience I gained of your professional abilities during the period you were engaged for the Company, in the matter of the Bankruptcy of their Agent in the north, that should this be so the post would be filled by a thoroughly competent, energetic, and discreet officer, and one from whom the Company would derive the greatest service.

I am, my dear Sir,
Yours very truly,
S. SWARBRICK,
General Manager.

H. W. NELSON, Esq.,
16, Martin's Lane,
Cannon Street.

From the **TRUSTEES OF THE BEDFORD CHARITIES.
AND MAYOR OF BEDFORD.**

BEDFORD SCHOOLS,
BEDFORD,
August 19th, 1873.

THE Trustees of the Bedford Charity have great
pleasure in certifying that Mr. H. W. NELSON, of the
firm of Lowless, Nelson, & Jones, was specially engaged
to defend the interests of the Bedford Charity against
the attack of the Endowed Schools' Commissioners, and
the Board of Trustees are very desirous of bearing their
witness to the very great professional skill and ability
displayed by Mr. NELSON in the conduct of their case,
and which resulted in a fair and satisfactory settlement
of a very important and difficult question.

Signed on behalf of the Board of Trustees,

F. THOS. YOUNG,
Mayor and Chairman.

From the Revd. **ST VINCENT BEECHEY. M.A.,** Canon of
Manchester. Rector of Hilgay. and Chaplain to the Earl
of Ellesmere

August 25th, 1873.

MY DEAR SIR,

I have very great pleasure in expressing my very
favourable opinion of your clever and gentlemanly
management of the somewhat difficult and delicate legal
matters relating to my executorship, and, indeed, of
all your other professional labours, of which I have now
for so many years been witness. I feel very sure that few
solicitors can be found possessing the peculiar qualifi
cations required for a great City Corporation in larger
measure than yourself, and I heartily hope you may
succeed in obtaining the appointment.

Yours very sincerely,

ST. VINCENT BEECHEY.

H. W. NELSON, Esqre.

From Vice-Admiral Sir H. M. DENHAM, F.R S., &c.

UNITED SERVICE CLUB,

PALL MALL, S.W.,

August 29th, 1873.

DEAR MR. NELSON,

Hearing that you are a Candidate for the Solicitor-ship of the Clothworkers' Company, and as I have experienced your very able professional abilities, I feel justified in adding my testimony and commendation to the many others your worth will have elicited.

Yours faithfully,

H. M. DENHAM,

Vice-Admiral.

From E. T. GOURLEY, Esqre. M.P. for Sunderland.

> SUNDERLAND,
> *August 16th, 1873.*

THIS is to certify that I have known MR. H. W. NELSON for several years, during which time he has conducted on my behalf very important legal business, to my entire satisfaction, and with credit to himself.

EDW. T. GOURLEY.

From J. HEYWOOD JOHNSTONE, Esqre.. B.A

UNITED UNIVERSITY CLUB,
PALL MALL EAST, S.W.,
19th August, 1873.

MY DEAR SIR,

I understand that you are a Candidate for the office of Solicitor to the Clothworkers' Company, and from what I can personally testify as to your zeal for your clients' interests, your ability in the management of landed property, and your thorough acquaintance with both the principles and practice of commercial law, I feel sure that should you obtain the appointment you would fill the post with advantage to the Company and (as in all other positions) with credit to yourself. With very kind regards,

I am, my dear Sir,
Faithfully yours,
J. H. JOHNSTONE, B.A., CANTAB.

H. W. NELSON, Esq.

From J. L. REED. Esqre.

DOWNHAM MARKET,
18th August, 1873.

MY DEAR SIR,

I am informed you are a Candidate for the post
of Solicitor to the Clothworkers' Company. Now, I do
not know that anything I can say will assist you in attain-
ing your object; but if, as a landowner of the county of
Norfolk, my stating that your able management of the
Woodhall Estate, under very difficult circumstances, for
several years past will assist you, I have much pleasure in
communicating it.

Your activity and legal acumen ought, I am sure, to
render you a most valuable Agent in anything you under-
take.

Wishing you success,
I remain,
Yours faithfully,
T. L. REED.

H. W. NELSON, Esq.

From **T. STEVENSON**, Esqre., Councillor.

NORTH STREET, RIPON,
August 20th, 1873.

DEAR SIR,

Having heard that you are a Candidate for the Solicitorship to the Worshipful Company of Clothworkers of the City of London I have great pleasure in testifying as to your abilities as a Solicitor.

During the agitation in our City, with regard to the Action of the Endowed Schools' Commissioners, with reference to our FREE GRAMMAR SCHOOL, no one could have more ably and zealously assisted us, and as a Member of the Grammar School Committee, I can truthfully state that should the Worshipful Company of Clothworkers enlist your services, they will have engaged one whom I believe will faithfully, fearlessly, and conscientiously do his duty.

Trusting you may be successful in your candidature,

I am,
Yours faithfully,
THOMAS STEVENSON.
Councillor.

H. W. NELSON, Esq.

From G. M HARVEY, Esqre.

THE PINES, STREATHAM HILL,
August 18th, 1873.

MY DEAR SIR,

I leave Town to-day for a few weeks, and will see you on my return. I hear you are a Candidate for the office of Solicitor to the Clothworkers' Company, and take this opportunity to wish you every success.

Judging by my experience of the professional skill with which you have acted for myself and family for so many years, I feel sure that there is no one better fitted for the post you are trying for, and I much hope that the Company may secure your services.

I am, my dear Sir,
Yours very sincerely,
G. M. HARVEY.

H. W. NELSON, Esq.

FROM

MERCHANTS, &c.

———•———

For convenience I have arranged the Signatures in Alphabetical order.

To Mr. H. W. Nelson,

    26, Martin's Lane,

        Cannon Street.

HAVING heard that you are a Candidate for the office of Solicitor to the Worshipful Company of Clothworkers, we can confidently bear testimony to your ability as a lawyer and a man of business, and recommend you as a most suitable person to fill such a position, and are certain that you would bring to the discharge of its duties not only legal knowledge, but a determination by all other means in your power to promote the interests of the Company.

Dated the 29th day of August, 1873.

BAKER & DANIELS	. 5, Fenchurch Street.
BARFF & CO. .	. 9, Fenchurch Street.
D. BARKER & CO.	. Lower Thames Street, and 34, Wapping.
W. BARTER & CO.	. 38, Gracechurch Street.
W. G. BARTLEET . .	. Pinner's Hall, Broad Street.
BASDEN, TOWNSEND, & CO.	11, Great Saint Helen's, and Lloyd's.
R. & G. BAYLIS . .	. 16, Botolph Lane.
JOHN BENNETT & CO.	. 43, Fish Street Hill.
J. O. BORRADALE & CO.	. 150, Leadenhall Street.

W. E. BOTT & CO. . . . 10, Mark Lane.
BULLIVANT & ALLEN . 114, Fenchurch Street.
CLOID, ROUTLEDGE, & CO. 5, East India Avenue.
COLLINGS & CO. . . . 3, Cross Lane.
J. COLMAN (J. & J. COLMAN) . 108, Cannon Street.
CRAVEN & CO. . . . 5, Great Saint Helen's.
W. CUNNINGHAM & CO. . 17, Gracechurch Street.
T. L. DEVITT (DEVITT &
 MOORE) . . . . . 109, Leadenhall Street.
H. W. EATON, M.P. for Coventry 33, Old Broad Street.
HENRY ELLIS & SONS . 17, Gracechurch Street.
WM. ELMSLIE & SON . . 12, Saint Michael's Alley, Cornhill.
EDWIN FOX & BOUSFIELD . 24, Gresham Street.
FULLER & FULLER . . 25, Bucklersbury.
HENRY GARBUTT . . Mark Lane and Chiswick.
HARRISON BROTHERS . 17, Gracechurch Street.
WM. HOOTEN & YATES . 12, Fenchurch Street.
J. D. HEWETT & CO. . . 3, Leadenhall Street.
W. & E. HUNT . . . White Lion Street.
JOHNSTON & SONS . 38, Botolph Lane.
A. JIMENEZ & SONS . 116, Fenchurch Street.
KEELING & HUNT . Monument Yard, &c.
T. C. LAURENCE . . 47, Lime Street.
H. R. LOMAS . . . East India Chambers.
GEO. LORAM & CO. . . 4, Cullum Street.
LISTER & BRIGGS . . 3, Laurence Pountney Lane.
LIVINGSTONE, BRIGGS, &
 CO. . . . . . 31. Great Saint Helen's.
ROBT. MACANDREW & CO. 2, Bond Court, Walbrook.
McGAVIN & CO. . . Barge Yard, Bucklersbury.
MILLS & MILNE . . . 27, Leadenhall Street.
MORICE & DIXEY . . 33, Cornhill, and Lloyd's.
MULLENS, MARSHALL, &
 DANIELL . . . . 4, Lombard Street.
JAMES NAVIN & CO. . . Bucklersbury.
JOHN PATTON, JUNR., & CO. 3, White Lion Court, Cornhill.
E. PELLAS & CO. . . 34, Fenchurch Street.

PETTY, WOOD, & CO. . . 13, King William Street.
JOHN PRESTON . . . 98, Gracechurch Street.
J. S. PROWSE, HALL, &
JEPSON . . . 17, Gracechurch Street.
REYNOLDS & EASON . . 43, Bishopsgate Street.
WM. RICHARDS & CO. . New City Chambers.
ROBINSON, FLEMING, & CO. 21, Austin Friars.
RUNCIMAN & SMITH . . 5, Laurence Pountney Lane.
SALCEDO & CO. . . . 9, Gracechurch Street.
SATOW, HITCHCOCK, & CO. Hercules Passage, Threadneedle
Street.
G. SEMENZA & CO. . . Gresham House.
SHARMAN BROTHERS . 27, Old Broad Street.
BRUNO, SILVA, & CO. . 35, Crutched Friars.
JAMES SLIM . . . . 17, Spital Square.
FREDK. B. SMART, SNELL,
& CO. . . . . . 85 & 86, Cheapside.
W. & J. SMITH . . . 106, Leadenhall Street.
M. W. THOMAS . . . 7, Austin Friars.
TOMLIN, KENDELL, & CO. . 33, Eastcheap.
J. WADDELL & CO. . . 7, Poultry.
WHITE BROTHERS . 25, Philpot Lane.
H. & J. WHITE . . 213, Shoreditch.
WIGHTMAN & CO. . . 19, Gracechurch Street.
WOODMAN & HAMBRIDGE . George Lane, Eastcheap.
H. P. WOOD . . . 3, New Square, Minories.

115, CITY ROAD,
LONDON,
14th August, 1873.

H. W. NELSON, ESQRE.,

DEAR SIR,

We are very pleased to hear that you contemplate offering yourself as a Candidate for the office of Solicitor to the Worshipful Company of Clothworkers.

May we be permitted to offer to those gentlemen on your behalf our testimony to the high opinion we have formed of your capabilities, both as a lawyer and a man of business? And we cannot but think that that ancient Company will be fortunate in securing the services of such an able gentleman, such an earnest advocate of the rights and welfare of City Guilds.

We are, dear Sir,
Faithfully yours,
CHAMPION & CO.

From SOLICITORS IN THE CITY OF LONDON.

To Mr. H. W. Nelson,
  26, Martin's Lane,
    Cannon Street.

From our professional connection with you, extending over a long period, we can confidently state we have always found you an honourable, upright, and able member of our profession, and always zealously devoted to the interests of your clients.

BANNISTER & ROBINSON.
R. & E. BASTARD.
CATTARNS, JEHU, & CATTARNS.
THOMAS COOPER.
HENRY C. COOTE.
DAVIDSONS, CARR. BANNISTER & MORRIS.
DYKE & STOKES.
ELLIS & CROSSFIELD.
J. A. FARNFIELD.
FIELDER & SUMNER.
GELLATLY, SON, & WARTON.
CHARLES P. GREENHILL.
W. HOUGHTON.
INGLE, COOPER, & HOLMES.
LEWIS & WATSON.
J. McDIARMID.
PARKER & CLARKE.
PLEWS & IRVINE.
PRITCHARD & SONS.
SIMPSON & CULLINGFORD.
STEVENS, WILKINSON, & HARRIES.
CYRUS WADDILOVE.
WALTONS, BUBB, & WALTON.
WESTALL, ROBERTS, & BARLOW.
ROBT. T. WRAGG.
YOUNG, MAPLES, TEESDALE, NELSON & CO.

www.ingramcontent.com/pod-product-compliance
Lightning Source LLC
Chambersburg PA
CBHW032141080426
42733CB00008B/1154